A Fairy Story *Come* True

Discovering the Afterlife Through Grieving

A.J. HARRISON

WESTBOW
PRESS
A DIVISION OF THOMAS NELSON

WestBow Press books may be ordered through booksellers or by contacting:

*WestBow Press
A Division of Thomas Nelson
1663 Liberty Drive
Bloomington, IN 47403
www.westbowpress.com
1-(866) 928-1240*

*ISBN: 978-1-4497-6838-6 (sc)
ISBN: 978-1-4497-6839-3 (e)*

Library of Congress Control Number: 2012921663

Printed in the United States of America

WestBow Press rev. date: 11/14/2012

— ❖ —

To my mother, Kathryn. Her departure from this life inspired this book. Her loving, generous nature inspired my spirit.

Special thanks to…

My Lord and Savoir, Jesus Christ

My God given family: my father, Bill, my sisters, Arika, Angela, and Arin, my brothers, Keenan and Louis, my nephew and nieces, Adriel, Jaiden, and Mariah.

My church family at Church on the Rock in St. Peters, MO.

You, the reader, thank you for having an open mind by opening this book. I pray that it blesses you, as God has blessed me to write it.

Special thanks to my editors Keenan E. Bull and Sarah L. Patton-Jamison

This book is not at all strictly for Christians, but for anyone who has found him or herself grieving the passing of a loved one and is curious and/or doubtful about the existence of the afterlife.

"I am the resurrection and the life; he who believes in Me will live even if he dies, and everyone who lives and believes in Me will never die . Do you believe this?" – **Jesus**

John 11:26 (NASB)

Contents

Introduction...

Growing up in the non-denominational Christian faith, I have known of the promise of God's Kingdom and eternal life to all who acknowledge Jesus Christ as their Lord and Savior since before I can remember. It is the ultimate goal in life for all Christians and we encourage everyone we encounter to strive for it. However, while living in these days and times where reality and porn stars get paid millions to chug beer at club openings while I spend my life savings (before I even had life savings) on college tuition, one might get their priorities a little twisted. I mean, I'm pretty sure I only earned one degree, but I'm pretty sure that I'm paying for at least two. When you look past all the rehab visits, "accidental" sex tapes, and DUIs of the rich and famous, you think to yourself, "how can I get some of that?!" And so, while I have never doubted the existence of a Heaven, I had never really given it much thought. I guess I kinda thought of it as something like, as people say, "I'll cross that bridge when I get to it." I wasn't really thinking a whole lot about death or what comes after it, because I always figured that there's plenty of time to worry about that later. Instead, I thought a lot more about a way to make money as fast and as easy as doing one of the sleazier reality shows, but a lot less mortifying.

It wasn't until March 21st, 2011, at about 8:45 a.m. that I would begin to truly observe the dimension of death. I saw that it was a portal to that ultimate goal of eternal life. But not for me; at least not at that time. The portal was for my mother, who had already gone through it by the time my father and I reached her hospital room. I had wondered before if I would immediately burst into tears the moment I realized one of my loved ones had been pronounced dead, like those "Oscar-worthy" scenes in movies. Though when I sat in the chair in front of the bed where her lifeless body laid, it took a little longer for me to cry than I had imagined. Of course I was in shock, but there was something else. Just like that, I received my revelation. Well, part of it anyhow. The rest would be revealed in the midst of my grieving.

What is this "Fairy Story" I speak of?

There are a few different reasons why I'm writing this. For one, like I said, Christians encourage *all* people to discover the Good News. That good news being that since Christ died for our sins we receive eternal life in God's kingdom, a.k.a. Heaven. And because life really sucks (yes, some of us Christians readily admit to this), many people have given up hope that there is a Kingdom of Heaven or a God that created it for that matter. One day, very recently after my mom's passing, I read a *CBS* news article[*] about the world renowned physicist and cosmologist Stephen Hawking. Hawking had stated that the concept of Heaven is a "fairy story" and that when people die they more or less just shut down like a computer or a piece of machinery. The article sincerely saddened me because I hate knowing that people think that the deplorable characteristics of this world are the only things that they'll ever get to experience. When you think about yourself, your loved ones, or anyone, in addition to all the bewildering energy and emotions our bodies encompass, could you really think that all of that just fizzles out once the body has deactivated? Dear Lord, I hope not, because that would mean that life *really, really,* sucks and then you just power down like a piece of junk! But since that isn't the case (and it isn't, with all due respect Mr. Hawking), that means that no one ever truly dies and the spirit lives on. And so, that being said, I want people to realize that life is but a backdrop to a stage play all about souls. Although this backdrop seems convincingly real, it is only the atmosphere in which our souls *temporarily* live. Hawking used the phrase "fairy story" to demean the afterlife as a childish or naïve concept. Well, I think I kind of like the afterlife being referred to as a fairy story; the Heavenly afterlife anyhow. I say this because the anticipation of an eternity of pure peace and joy is just as enchanting as a fairy tale. Sort of like the princess awaiting her prince to rescue her. I also just like taking offensive comments and altering them to compliment my own ideas!

This is how Heaven works, this Bible passage, John 1:9-13 (NIV), summarizes Jesus' nature, His life here on earth, and His role in our achievement of the Kingdom of Heaven: [9] *"The true light that gives light to everyone was coming into the world.* [10] *He was in the world, and though the world was made through Him, the world did not recognize Him.* [11] *He came to that which was His own, but His own did not receive him.* [12] *Yet to all who did receive Him, to those who believed in His name, He gave the right to become children of God—* [13] *children born not of natural descent, nor of human decision or a husband's will, but born of God."*

- Morgan, D. (2011, May 17). Stephen Hawking: Heaven is "a fairy story". *CBSNews, World Watch*. Retrieved from http://www.cbsnews.com/8301-503543_162-20063168-503543.htm

The second reason I'm writing this is because it's therapeutic. I'm still grieving my mother's passing. Though I believe in a happier afterlife for both her and myself, I don't deny myself the expression of grief. Outside of suicide or any other destructive behavior, I don't believe there's a wrong way to grieve. However, my revelation of the connection of life, death, and the afterlife has been a great source of ease for my grieving. I fully understand that grieving is very complicated and not at all easy. We go through highs and lows, we never know when it's gonna hit, or how long it'll take before the next emotion takes over. But I know that if I didn't have my belief in God and His promises that my grieving would be a lot more difficult. I never would've imagined that I could feel as normal and happy as I so often have so soon after the passing of any of my loved ones. In fact, it's downright bizarre.. I simply do not know how people can go through grieving without this hope.

But we do not want you to be uninformed, brethren, about those who are asleep, so that you will not grieve as do the rest who have no hope.- 1 Thessalonians 4:13 (NASB)

— ❃ —

How it all happened...

People often say *how* and *when* your loved one died can have an influence on how you grieve. If they were elderly and or sick, it doesn't necessarily make the grieving process easier but we may be able to accept it faster because that person will no longer suffer with ailments. Sometimes this is the case. Let's keep it real. When your 80 year old great aunt or uncle moves on from this life it just isn't as sad as when your friend died in their 20s or 30s. Nonetheless you'll miss anyone that is dear to you and there usually is some element to their passing that makes it seem untimely. Maybe they were sick but young. Maybe they were older but never seemed happy and you wish they could've experienced better days before they'd left. Maybe they were old enough and often happy, but their passing has caused financial or social issues amongst you and your family. These types of thoughts and feelings make grieving difficult. As for me, my mother was only 56. That was something I detested immediately. Being a registered nurse in the neo-natal intensive care unit at a children's hospital, she worked too much and was tired and sick *all* the time. This made me angry too. Both her illness and death were avoidable. This…really ticked me off. I concentrated on these things in the second and third week after she passed. The first week I was almost paralyzed from the pain. It's like when you're in enormous, physical pain and you don't want to move around too much for fear that you'll feel it even more. So once I regained normal, physical feeling, that's when the anger poured in. It just didn't seem fair! Not to me or anyone else in our family.

My mom, Kathryn, raised four daughters: Arika, Angela, Arin, and myself. She was married to our father, Bill, worked more than full time as a nurse, and cared for her ailing mother all at once. She was a dominant personality and so she ran the household. With an iron fist I might add. She paid the bills, made household decisions, cooked meals, picked us up from school, and handled any disciplinary issues. All of this contributed to her exhaustion. She insisted on doing it all because she wanted to do things her way. She was also overly generous. The way I've described her for years is that she was a person who'd give you the shirt off her back, but God help you if you didn't wear that shirt the way she told you to wear it! Over the years she temporarily cured her exhaustion with an unhealthy diet that she likely felt gave her an instant energy boost. Also, her family came from rural Mississippi, and I'm pretty sure that animals are born fried there, she didn't have chance. Unfortunately the fried, heavy and over-seasoned foods turned into diabetes. Diabetes turned into heart disease and heart disease turned into kidney failure. Since all of these diseases are commonly manageable, Kathryn refused to stop working, which worsened her symptoms.

My family had been concerned about my mom's health for at least seven years. Her energy levels dropped, she became weak and fragile, and her weight fluctuated dramatically. The diabetes was disheartening but considering we had several other diabetic relatives on her side of the family it didn't seem to be a health condition that would be intractable. After my freshman year in college, I prepared to leave town to do an internship. One night just a couple of weeks prior to my leaving, my Dad woke me up out of my sleep and told me that my mom's job had called and said that she had fallen at work and was being taken to the hospital.

It was then that we discovered she had suffered a mild heart attack. I reluctantly left town soon after she was released from the hospital. When I returned months later she appeared delightfully healthy and was practicing a healthier lifestyle. Somewhere along the way, however, that healthy lifestyle started to slack off. Fast forward four years, and Kathryn is still working. She walks with the posture of someone 20 years her senior and I, more or less, had become her care taker. Still in college, I stayed at home and assisted her with daily activities including grocery shopping and doctor's appointments. It was bitter sweet. I hated her being sick but it gave us an incredible bond. We spent pretty much everyday together. No matter how hard it was, I felt that it was a blessing that I could be there for her.

Arriving to the hospital for an appointment one day, she felt so bad that I wheeled her up to the office. I was terrified when the nurse returned to the waiting room to speak with me without her. The nurse told me that the doctor wanted to send her to the emergency room. This was when things got *really* scary. After a hellish night in the E.R. she was diagnosed with kidney failure. Her doctor frankly stated that if she hadn't come in that day she would've died within the next three days. Mom then began dialysis treatments at a clinic. For the first couple of months or so she seemed better. She was on a leave of absence and was on a strict renal diet. Although, with the consent of her doctors, she went back to work. Ignoring and disputing all the pleas of her family, she went back to work. Let me remind you that this was no desk job. This was a matter of life and death, do or die job. It was just too much. Her body couldn't handle the combination of dialysis treatments and work. Once she grew tired of going to the clinic, she decided that she wanted to be trained to do home dialysis. Without ever asking my opinion, she called upon me to sign off as her "partner" in home dialysis. Three to four days a week, I stood there in my face mask and gloves, looking at this machine with several blinking lights, buttons, numbers, and tubes of overwhelming proportion thinking to myself "I can't do this." The machine was a monster. It sounded alarms continually, and consistently scared the crap out of both of us because we knew that if the slightest mistake took place she could die. She was in constant pain, discomfort, and stress and I was in constant worry and stress. It was a rare relief when we got through a treatment without something going wrong.

On a Friday night, I prepared to unhook her from the machine when we discovered that the cap to the catheter in her chest (connected to her heart) was stuck. I called in my sister Arika and my father to help and no one could remove it. I felt as horrible as I did helpless as I watched her wince from pain every time we twisted the cap. We actually had to use pliers to finally twist it off. However, the fact that we used pliers on the catheter to her very heart concerned us that she might have contracted an infection in her bloodstream. So we hurried to the E.R. I walked with her arm-in-arm as I so often did to balance her. I felt how tragically fragile she was. Every move was unbearable, I could tell. She was even having trouble signing herself in at the desk, so I did it for her. In reflection it is notable that even through all of this I was still only a little concerned. Mom's health scares had become an ill-fated norm and besides, we had faith that everything would be fine. If there was anything that mom had driven into my head, it was to have faith that everything would be fine "In Jesus' name." They kept her overnight to be sure that everything was okay. We kissed her goodnight and had a couple of laughs with her and went home because she looked much better.

The next morning, we came to check her out of the hospital. The rest of the family, my other two sisters, their husbands, and my niece and nephew gathered at our house to welcome her home. Though everyone had become accustomed to the scares, we never missed an opportunity to get together and rejoice about the positive outcome. As most everyone left following the brief gathering, my mom dreadfully went over to the dialysis machine to begin a scheduled treatment. The first steps of the treatments were the most difficult. So I usually let her do that part on her own so as to not mess anything up. After all, she was the nurse. I always stood or sat near by just in case she needed me. This time I was a lot more relaxed. I was still tired from waiting in the E.R. all night so I slouched on the couch behind her. She started screwing on a syringe to her catheter when she dropped the syringe. She said to me, "Hand me that," and I simultaneously got up and picked it up. Wearing a face mask and a pair of gloves she reached out to the other syringes hanging from the machine and asked me for one of them. When I gave her the new syringe she fastened it onto her catheter and slowly backed down into the chair right behind her. Her eyes glared at the floor as her body became limp. Thinking that this was another case of "low blood pressure," I quickly grabbed some of the boxes of medical equipment and tried to prop her feet up on them. I screamed for my sister Arika and she called 911. The emergency operator told us to lay her on the floor as Arika began to administer CPR. I cradled my mother's head in my hands. I placed one hand behind her head and one hand over her forehead as I prayed in her ear and assured her that everything would be fine. Her eyes glared at the ceiling now as she made long, drastic gasps for breath. She had gone into cardiac arrest. The paramedics stabilized her and whisked her off to the E.R., only two hours after she had checked out of the hospital.

After a somewhat calm wait in the E.R. waiting room, my dad called Arika and me back into the room to see her. Little did I know that when I walked into that room, I would never be the same. My life would never be the same. My family would never be the same. Her eyes weren't at all focused. They dashed all around the room. She wouldn't respond to Arika. I myself, could not bare to try to communicate with her. She had lost oxygen to her brain. I had never been so hurt in my life.

Later they sent her to the Intensive Care Unit where my father, sisters, brothers, and I would spend the next week waiting and praying for her to wake up, to talk to us, or even just look at us. There was no peaceful zone. Being in the room with her was hopeless because she wasn't mentally present and being in the waiting room was turmoil as the families of other patients cried out in distress. Now, I've never been on a battle field and I've never been to prison, but the waiting room of a Intensive Care Unit has *got* to be one of the worst places on earth. I not only felt my own sorrow, but the pain of everyone around me. These complete strangers became familiar faces that waited all day every day for the same reason, to find out if their loved one was going to die. My fellow mourners were from all walks of life. People of all ages, gender, and ethnicities are stripped of our barriers and our "oh-so-important" agendas when dealing with death. *No one* escapes it.

Throughout the week mom got better. They turned down her breathing machine and some of the doctors and nurses offered the hope that she could possibly walk out of the hospital. However, by the next Friday her doctors explained that she had experienced irreversible neurological damage and that after another week they would take her off of all life support. Until that moment I had never felt completely hopeless. I'd never felt so distant from God. It wasn't out of spite or because of my disappointment, but only that I didn't feel that He was there. I felt like my family and I were alone. I had always thought that we were immune to tragedy. Okay, I'll admit it. I even thought we were immune to death. I assumed that since the world was getting crappier by the day that we all would be gracefully raptured and not have to experience the calamity of death. After all, isn't death, like, the worst thing that could happen to anyone? The thought is instilled in us from the time we're old enough to know what death is. Alive-good, dead-bad. I would soon discover a different aspect of death. Although, at this time, it was the worst thing that could happen.

On Sunday I went to church blubbering and my "church family" created a circle as we prayed in agreement that my mother would be healed. I felt God's presence again as I was completely sure that she would pull through. I was still distraught but I felt much better. The next morning the hospital called and said that we should come. I already knew, because my mom had before told me that nurses never tell you that your loved one has died over the phone. They just tell you that you need to be there. She looked asleep but not at all present.

And so, how and why mom passed was at first a problem for me. I had thoughts like, "I should've expressed to her more that I didn't want her to work," or "did I do something wrong during that last dialysis treatment?" These ideas could haunt me for life if I allowed them to. And for anyone who has guilt or regret over how their loved one passed, I know it sounds too easy to just not allow the thoughts to come to you. My faith that my mother is in heaven and that all is well with her, permits me to rid myself of any guilt. Think about this: whatever happened or whatever you think should have happened, your loved one is supposed to be where they are right now. You can depend on God's sovereignty. I think that it is helpful to talk with someone about what you think should have or could have happened in the past for your own release, and after that, you should try to let it go. Guilt is nothing but a cruel form of self torture. Nothing will torment you more.

So, how are you grieving?

Now that you're over your past regrets, how are you doing? "Take it one day at a time" was the phrase I heard most at my Mom's funeral. Friends and family said it. I'd heard it before then and never *truly* knew what the heck it meant. I finally understood it when I woke up one day and realized that I had a lot on my agenda. I welcomed the full day because I knew that it would help me to not think of mom so much and it did. Before I knew it the day was over. It was a pretty good day too and as I went to bed I thought, "This wasn't so bad." So I prayed to God to make the next day as easy, and the next day and the next day. Still, when I wake up, I think of her and then I think, "I know that I can get through today without her. All I need is God…and a little coffee." Before, I was driving myself crazy thinking way down the road about all the things that I was going to absolutely hate doing without her. Everything from my wedding day (I'm not engaged, but *every* girl dreams okay) to going through childbirth. My head was spinning out of control in horrible sadness. But now, I stop myself every time and I think "take it one day at a time." Heck, take it minute by minute!

Now, of course, not every day is easy. I'll honestly say that most are, but certainly not all days. And yes, you need to allow yourself some leeway. Anyone who doesn't sympathize with you, tell 'em to can it (unless it's your boss, a police officer, or anyone else who could cause you trouble). What you're going through is one of the most traumatic things a person can experience and you simply don't have time for people who don't understand that. You can't be strong all of the time.

My family has developed its own way of communicating. As soon as my mom passed we started telling each other that we need "a moment," meaning we are about to cry. Or we may say "I had a bad moment this morning" or ask "Are you about to have a moment?" Under the conditions a mourner is in, it is absolutely rude to try to disrupt a person's moment. If that is how they feel at that time let them have their moment, even if you are trying to eat or watch t.v. This can be difficult when you're feeling pretty okay at that moment and would like to stay that way, but you have to be there for them. Scripture commands us to: *"rejoice with those who rejoice, and weep with those who weep and be of the same mind toward one another."* – Romans 12:15-16 (NKJV)

If you are also mourning you have the same right. There is no schedule to grieving so you just have to ride each moment out. You can't postpone it. I still live with my dad at my parent's house, meaning I still live where my mom went into cardiac arrest in the living room, where all of her favorite movies on DVD are always visible through the glass of the entertainment center, where I walk into her kitchen that has a sign saying "Grandma's kitchen" that I don't have the heart to take down, and where her makeup and perfumes are still in her bathroom. It's but a wonder that I'm not in a moment 24 hours a day! But I'm not; because I got rid of what I knew would bother me and kept what didn't. I keep everything that reminds me of her good and fun characteristics and memories. As for the stuff I got rid of? Everything that reminded me of how sick she was had to go. The syringes, gloves, face masks, the medication, and that atrocious dialysis machine. I would've kicked that piece of crap off of a cliff if I knew where one was in this state (I'm not very adventurous). Also, along with my sister Arika, my dad and I replaced the rug where she laid that night. "You do what you gotta do" to help yourself get through your everyday life.

Hey, you're still living you know...

Alright, after you've had your moment, you'll likely feel better. So please, if you're okay, do yourself a favor and let yourself be okay! It isn't going to seem like you're over your loved one's passing too soon if someone catches you at the movies or cracking a joke over Facebook. If other people seem to feel like you're over your loved one's passing too soon, so what?! Grieving hurts so bad that if you have a day or some times when you don't feel it, enjoy. You'll appreciate these good moments when the bad ones come around again. So don't sit there trying to make yourself cry by listening to one of those really depressing Carol King or James Taylor songs. *You know* what I'm talking about!

During my first week of mourning, I was so distraught that I stayed at my sister Angela's house (for fear of going home to a Kathryn-less house) for four days wearing a hoodie that I refused to take off. I thought that I would be a basket-case forever. Then, I had a moment of relief. While I was sitting on the couch my darling little nieces and nephew got out the game *Candy Land**. My other sister Arin hopped down on the floor and shouted "Who wants to play?!" My first thought was, "how could I play a game right now?" but somehow my playful side fought its way to the front and before I knew it I was plunking down on the floor yelling "I do!!!" It was like someone had pushed play on my life. I lost miserably…to three kids, but it was the best game of Candy Land *ever*. Later I told Angela, "this is still life, and it's still a good one."

**Candyland*, Property of *Hasbro*

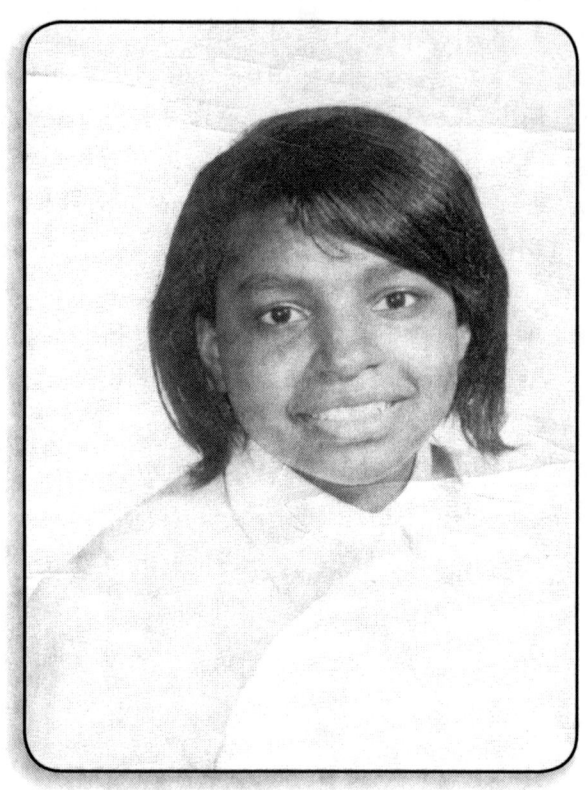

Middle school photo of Kathryn.

*Kathryn at her 21st Birthday Party
with then boyfriend, Bill.*

College of Nursing Graduation photo.

Family photo, from left: Arika, A.J. (me),
Kathryn, Bill, Angela, and Arin.

Kathryn and Bill on Christmas. Mom and
dad were married for 31 years and just two weeks
from their 32nd anniversary when she passed.

With the grandkids, from left:
Mariah, Adriel, and Jaiden.

"Grandma's Kitchen!" Kathryn cooks
while grandson Adriel closely observes.

From left: Kathryn, A.J., Arin, Angela, and Arika cooking and chatting in Angela's kitchen.

Me and Mom at a dinner party.

—— ❋ ——

What you can take from the experience of grieving...

There is a sentence you will always hear at a funeral. "LIFE IS SHORT." I've never heard a eulogy that did not include this sentence or some alternative of it and I think I've been to twice as many funerals than weddings now. Nearly every eulogy uses this phrase because it's oh so true. However, when people hear a phrase over and over again it tends to lose its sting over time. So I've adopted my sister Angela's version of the age-old saying, "Life is but a glimpse." I repeat these words to myself to keep myself from freaking out over stupid stuff (i.e. someone not responding to my voice/ text message) and to keep myself in check about what is truly important in life. Our short life span is brought up at funerals usually to induce an altar call. When someone dies people suddenly remember that well...we die. Everybody wants to know what happens after death and particularly what will happen after *their own* death, whether they'll admit it or not. So, if you hadn't already given thought to your life after death and how your lifestyle now will affect your hereafter, take the experience of grieving as an opportunity for a new awakening. Like I said earlier, I was raised in the church, so my general belief system has never changed. But the connection between my belief system and my lifestyle has absolutely changed. I have tuned out society and tuned into God. Everything that used to matter doesn't and everything that didn't matter as much before does. Losing 15 pounds before the next party I go to-- not important anymore. Making sure I don't have to work on the days I go to church-- definitely important. People are always looking for a basis for their life, something to refer back to, look forward to, or consult when making an important decision. That basis could be their career, social life, or image/reputation-- all things that don't last. Your salvation that you receive through Christ? That lasts for an eternity; make that your deciding factor...for everything. You don't want to waste your life on the meaningless, remorseless and degrading practices of this world. Humbling yourself to live for God will balance everything for you in this unbalanced world.

Whereas you do not know what *will happen* tomorrow. For what *is* your life? It is even a vapor that appears for a little time and then vanishes away. - James 4:14 (NKJV)

I often look around at my mom's personal items and think about the verse 1Timothy 6:7 *"For we have brought nothing into the world, so we cannot take anything out of it either."* Her things mean a lot to me because they remind me of her. I'm extra careful with them because they were her things, but really that's just it, they're things. As she resides in perfect peace, she herself cares nothing, and I do mean nothing, about her old things. We cling to our "things" so tightly throughout life. Its always, "I forgot my things!" "Stay out of my things!" "Those are my things!" God forbid, if any disaster ever hit your house. No matter what type of person you are, eventually you would say, " what about my things?!" or "my things were in there!" So, I think a lot about how I anticipate leaving my things behind one day. As much as I adore them now, I can imagine the bliss of chucking everything without a single care. In fact, I'm so excited I'm starting early! Now, I'm not talking about throwing my belongings away. You'd probably find me on the floor in fetal position 15 minutes after I threw my iPod away. What I mean is that I've started to see my things for the simple material that they are. It's okay for you to have things, nice things. God wants us to have things to comfort us during our lifetime. But remember that your clothes, electronics, transportation, residence, etc., and the money you spent to get them are all passing *things* that someday you'll have to leave behind. So while its quite alright to spend time shining the rims of your favorite car, furnishing your house, or shopping for clothes (this would be me all the way), you might just wanna use most of your precious time primping and fortifying your soul. I'm just sayin.

Your experience of grieving can also improve your relationship with people. One never realizes just how insensitive or inconsiderate he/she has been until he/she is the one in need. Before my mom passed, I always felt sorry for anyone who had to bury a close loved one, just as any warm-blooded being should. Though truthfully, I rarely gave the person or persons in mourning a second thought after the funeral. Not very long after mom's funeral, I realized how this happens. I'm not saying that people don't really mean it when they say "I'm so sorry" or "Let me know if you ever need anything." Well, actually, I usually question the sincerity of the "Let me know if you ever need anything," because though people really may be sorry about what you're going through, most people don't entail other people's problems or situations into their everyday schedule. They think, "I showed up, I hugged you, I sent you a card and flowers, now if you'd excuse me I need to stop at Wal-Mart on the way home." Don't get me wrong, everyone's life is supposed to go on after a funeral, so don't be mad if you've stopped receiving the cards, care packages, and the "just checking in on you" phone calls within the next couple of weeks afterwards. My point is that now that you've felt what it's like to be the person in grieving, you can be that exceptional person who actually does call to just check in on someone who is grieving *months* after the funeral. Never having been much on conversation or "touchy-feely-ness," I really do feel comforted when people take the time to talk with me about how I or my family is doing. You'll be a blessing to someone who is hurting when you ask them how they're doing, or let them reminisce with you about their loved one, or even share with them about how you've been dealing with grieving as well. And yes, hugs are awesome too! You'll be guaranteed a spot on someone's "most caring people list" for sure. Comforting people in their time of need, whether it is due to a loss or any other hapless event, will count towards bettering your lifestyle in preparation for your afterlife. Jesus' command for us to care for one another, as He stated in John 13:34 *"A new command I give you: Love one another. As I have loved you, so you must love one another,"* is expressed numerous times throughout the Gospels. Outside of the Ten Commandments, it is the next, enormously important commandment for us to follow. We must take the well being of others into consideration. Probably more often than you'd like to think. Making ourselves reliable for others helps to eliminate our selfishness and impatience, making us all around better people. I know this is easier said than done because some may not always be appreciative of your efforts and some people are, lets say, extra needy.

"Blessed be the God and Father of our Lord Jesus Christ, the Father of mercies and God of all comfort, who comforts us in all our affliction so that we will be able to comfort those who are in any affliction with the comfort with which we ourselves are comforted by God." -2 Corinthians 1:3-4 (NASB)

You may also learn something about yourself through all of this. You can discover your capability to love unconditionally. Just think about it. When we mourn someone's absence we're expressing a desire for that person's presence even though not every moment with them was ideal. Even if you often fought with them, you'd rather them be here because you love them. You know who else loves unconditionally? God of course! Bet you didn't see that one coming. And it was He that instilled that sense of love in you. So, even though your loved one has already gone on before you, you can apply your unconditional love to the people who are still here with you.

Outside of my ability to love unconditionally, I discovered my own faith through grieving. In the days of waiting in the Intensive Care Unit with my mom, my family and I also awaited the results of tests they conducted to test her brain function. After a couple of days none of her doctors even mentioned the results. In anticipation, my sister Arika found one of the doctors and bluntly asked her about the results. The doctor, usually being blunt herself, said that our mother wasn't brain dead and that she believed that she would walk out of the hospital one day. We talked with a nurse that was giving dialysis to mom and she also stated that she believed that she would wake up normal. For us, this was confirmation that she would be fine. This was the answer to our prayers. But then, a day later, her doctors called a meeting with us and told us that if she woke up her brain would not likely function normally because she had suffered irreversible brain damage. They said that if she did not show greater signs of both independent heart and brain function, that they would cease all forms of life support within ten days. They gave us the choice to end her life then or to wait the ten days. My dad requested they give her the ten days.

The day she passed wasn't the worst day of my life. *This* was the worst day of my life. Hearing the doctors predict such a horrible future for my mother and our family made me yearn to be sedated. As I stated earlier, I later felt reassured yet again that she would live and live well after praying at church the day before she passed. It was an emotional rollercoaster in every sense of the phrase. And so for weeks even after her passing, I questioned God on this. I thought, "Why did You make us believe that everything was going to be fine when it wasn't?! Why toy with our emotions?" I would reflect on how positive and sure I felt the day before she passed and how I literally could feel my faith as I couldn't before. This made me mad. I could see how God brings good out of every bad situation before, but not this. So I kept asking Him, "Why did You build up our hope?" Well, I got my answer. I got to see for myself that I could have faith in God no matter how bad the situation looked. The situation that I was in was down right ugly. It looked and felt hopeless. I had medical professionals telling me in other words that things were bad. Yet still, I went to church, I prayed, and I believed. My God, did I believe, with all my heart. It didn't turn out the way I had hoped and prayed. But you know that faith that I said I felt that day? It never went away. I don't know why it was best for my mom to pass away when she did or how she did. I have faith in God's mercy and I believe that He had mercy on us all that day. I believe that no prayer goes unanswered. It's the answer itself that's the mystery. The answer doesn't always match our idea of what the answer should be. But believe me, every prayer gets answered.

Because of God's mercy we did not have to make the dreaded decision to let her go. She let go on her own. We didn't even have to wait the ten days. We also didn't have to face the possibility of nursing home visits or 24 hour care if she had lived and neither did she. Being in that state would've been just as painful for her as it would've been for us.

Less than two months afterwards, I found myself closely observing a very similar situation with a friend of mine from college who had lived with cystic fibrosis all his life. I got a message from his wife stating that she and his mother were waiting about a week to discontinue his life support. I prayed that entire week (literally) that God would show his wife and their family the same mercy He had on my family by letting him pass on his own. The next week, I found out that they had to let him go. Even then, I still didn't doubt God's mercy. However our loved ones pass on from this life isn't going to be easy, because life isn't *ever* easy and the timing will *never* seem right. But you have to see His mercy in every situation. His mercy began when He graced your life with your loved ones' presence.

His mercy continues as He enables you to live on without having to worry about them any longer.

"...you will grieve, but your grief will be turned into joy." — **Jesus**, John 16:20 (NASB)

The fairy-story-come-true will put Disney World to shame...

L ike I once was, some people are so preoccupied with life that they don't give much profound thought to Heaven but do acknowledge that there is one. Some people don't care (or at least they say they don't but they really do). Then there are the people who believe that there is a Heaven and do think about it but are a little intimidated by the thought of actually going. I could once relate to this too and I believe the problem is that our earthly life is all that we know. There may be horrible acts of crime and injustice around every corner, but goshdarnit, this is "home." It is also understandable how the idea of literally floating or ascending upwards to an entirely different environment, or world if you will, could freak somebody out. The idea seems very Sci-Fi

Fantasy. Then there's also that key word that is used so often when describing Heaven, eternity, really... eternity? We have a hard enough time sitting in our cars awaiting the #4 combo which we already know isn't going to have extra mayo like we asked. How could we possibly ever wrap our minds around doing *anything* for eternity? It is hard to imagine, but that's just the thing, we won't know until we get there because Heaven is unimaginable. God's time is not equivalent to our concept of time.

The appearance of Heaven or God's Kingdom is also unimaginable. Though it is described in scripture, the description is so amazing that you still can't mentally grasp it. When I think of the fantastic environment of Heaven, I can't help but to think about how crazy people are about Disney World. People of all ages, ethnicity, and of both genders, have this bewildering, brain-washed-like fascination with Disney and its theme parks. Having once been an employee (or "cast member") at Disney World, I have personally witnessed the hypnotic allures of this legendary theme park. The secret of Disney Company leaders is that they're detail-oriented. Around every single corner there's some sort of sparkle, music, or lighting to keep people in ecstasy. I mean, they actually built the place so that you'd have to take a ferry boat to get there, hence the feeling of traveling to another world. And so

I think, "If man can create a place so seemingly perfect that people will work overtime just to spend their family vacation there, then Heaven must be Disney World on steroids!" God is detail-oriented too. There is a description of Heaven's nature in Revelation 21:19-21 (NIV), *"The foundations of the city walls were decorated with every kind of precious stone. The first foundation was jasper, the second sapphire, the third agate, the fourth emerald, [20] the fifth onyx, the sixth ruby, the seventh chrysolite, the eighth beryl, the ninth topaz, the tenth turquoise, the eleventh jacinth, and the twelfth amethyst.[f] [21] The twelve gates were twelve pearls, each gate made of a single pearl. The great street of the city was of gold, as pure as transparent glass."*

Disney World is not perfect by any means but they sure do try to give you the illusion that it is. So, it's a pleasure to even try to imagine a place that truly is perfect and 100% happy. In God's Kingdom, negative, tormenting feelings are ostracized. *"… Behold, the tabernacle of God is among men, and He will dwell among them, and they shall be His people, and God Himself will be among them, and He will wipe away every tear from their eyes; and there will no longer be any death; there will no longer be any mourning, or crying, or pain; the first things have passed away."* -Revelation 21:3-4 (NASB)

Now, even in some of your fondest memories, have you ever had a single day when everything was absolutely, positively, perfect? If you answered yes, I'll give you a moment to admit that you are lying. Things that are supposed to be perfect or even seem to be perfect in this life are not. Just try to recall something "perfect" in your life and you'll remember that there was some sort of damper involved, even the slightest thing. It was nice until... it stormed and the power went out, or [fill in name] got drunk and started a fight, the fire alarm went off, I had a cold, or I wish [fill in name] could have been there, I spilled punch on my shirt, etc. Not that we shouldn't make the most of could've-been-perfect times, because we'd be miserable if we didn't. But, wouldn't you like to experience pure, genuine perfection if you could?

In conclusion…

Writing a book about Heaven called "A Fairy Story Come True…" and then comparing it to Disney World could make some people believe even less in an afterlife. And yet, I'll take it a step further. One of the key words that both Disney leaders and cast members use continually is *believe*. They ask their young guests if they believe in magic and/or fairies and after the fireworks show comes to an end you hear the eerie whisper of a child asking "Do you believe?" They want you or at least your kids to actually believe that magic created this wondrous world of Disney. And while I write this book, I sometimes feel as if I'm taking on a very similar task. I am pleading with you to believe as much as I do in a God so loving that He will rescue us from the pains and hardship of this life and launch us into another life of eternal peace and joy no matter how far-fetched it seems. Spreading the good news of the Kingdom of Heaven is becoming more hopeless by the year. With the increase and rapid evolution in technological devices used for the purposes of science, medicine, marketing, socializing, and entertainment, more and more people are putting their belief into themselves. We try to solve everything ourselves and therefore we think we've got it all figured out. And I believe that most people don't even realize it. All the answers that we think we need just appear on the screen before us. There seems to be a quick and easy solution to every element of labor in our everyday lives, to the point where it's as if all we have to do now is live. But how many of us really know how to do that? And how many of us know what to live life for?

I think that people live to be happy. Everybody wants to be happy in one way or another and what we do in life is what we hope will result in a happily ever after. Our own special route to happiness varies greatly from working one job for money to open a coffee shop, to auditioning for roles to achieve fame, to studying foreign languages in order to travel the world, to stealing a car to sell its parts for drug money (hey, I said it varies). Whatever it may be, we do what we do from year to year, day to day, minute by minute because we think that it'll lead up to the grand finale. The problem? Most of our ideas of happiness not only don't prevail, but they often wind up hurting us along the way. Our ideas of what happiness is can lead to jail time, disease, debt, dysfunction amongst family or spouses, or death. Money can either be lost or stolen, marriage can easily be unraveled, fame fades, sex is unfulfilling, parties end, and alcohol or drug-fueled highs decline. In Matthew 24:35 (NASB), Jesus makes it clear that nothing in this life will last. That is with the exceptions of He Himself and our very souls. *"Heaven and earth will pass away, but My words will not pass away."*

No matter the amount of strife and pure annoyance I endure due to my fellow man, I sincerely want nothing more than to live with them in the harmony that will only exist in Heaven. So I apologize to any children, beauty pageant contestants, or hippies when I say this: There is no such thing as peace on Earth. Not in this lifetime. People are just too complicated and ill-natured to come to any sort of agreement of peace and that is why the world is what it is…horrendous. I wouldn't want anyone to go through the trials of this life only to spend eternity in more pain in the darkness of Hell. Yes, Hell, it may sound utterly ridiculous to most people nowadays, but you will either go to Heaven or Hell. As much as people would like to believe it, there is no in between. God isn't indecisive.

I have actually given a thought to the possibility of being wrong about the afterlife. I came to the conclusion that if I was wrong, I'd rather spend my life childishly believing in such a wonderful lie than to die knowing that I didn't live for something better than this life. However now, I not only believe, but I know. I will continue to spend my life in anticipation to meet my glorious Maker. I look forward to seeing my mother again. I think about how I'll walk with her arm-in-arm again, not to hold her up due to her weakness, but simply to walk with my mother, my sister in Christ in fellowship over those long-promised streets of gold.

CPSIA information can be obtained at www.ICGtesting.com
Printed in the USA
LVOW060046051212

309923LV00001B/13/P